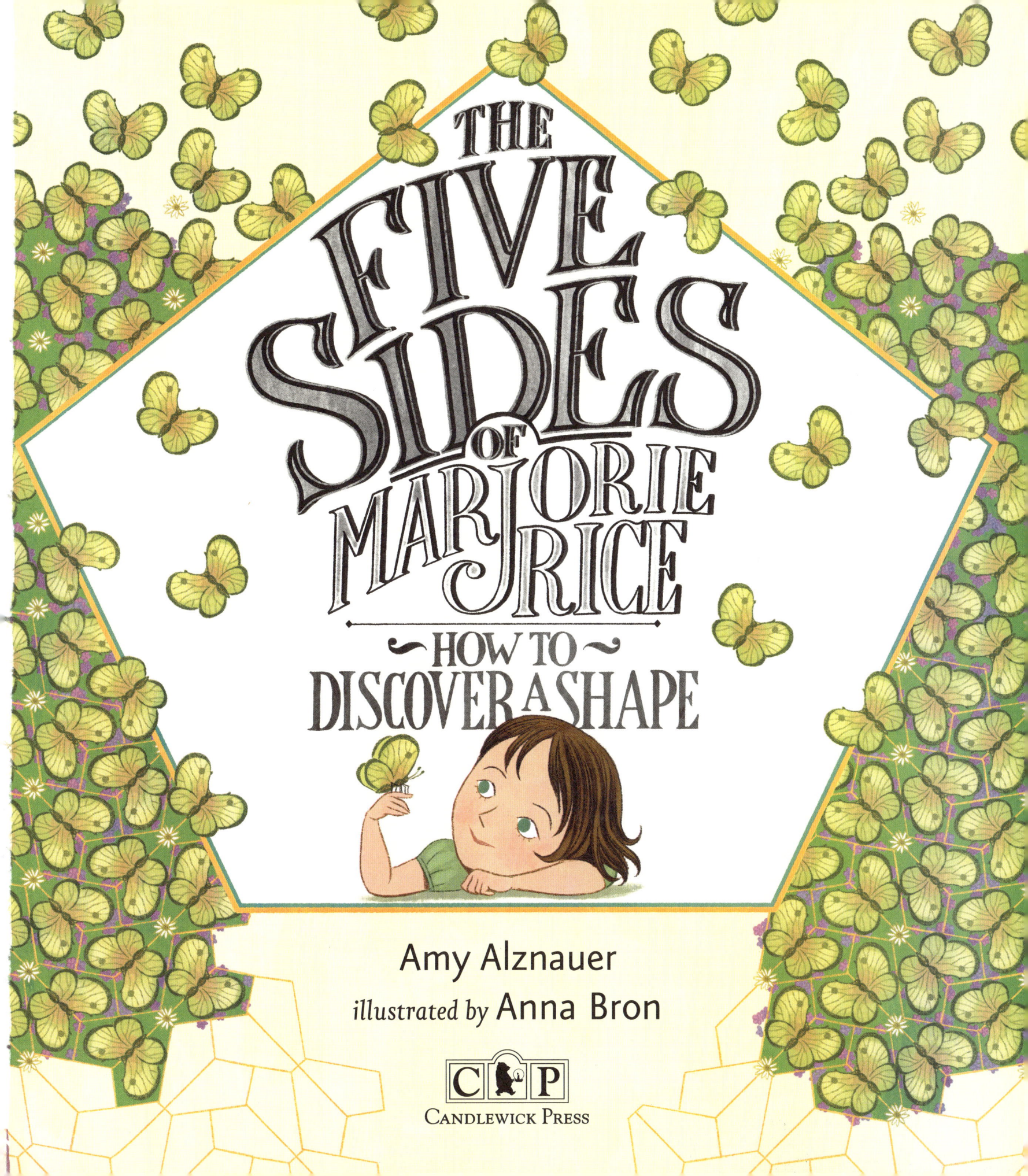

THE FIVE SIDES OF MARJORIE RICE

HOW TO DISCOVER A SHAPE

Amy Alznauer

illustrated by Anna Bron

CANDLEWICK PRESS

"Many of us are mathematicians just waiting to be born."
—Sunil Singh on Marjorie Rice

This is the story of a puzzle as old as mammoths
and a girl who grew up to astonish everyone by solving it.

But like a puzzle, a story often takes a long time
before all the pieces begin to fit.

Roseburg, Oregon, 1930s

When Marjorie was little, she looked for patterns everywhere, especially in the wild.

Swimming in the Umpqua River, her body became a shape in the water, the water a shape in the hills, and the hills a shape in the sky. Everything was filled in and around with something.

Long before there was writing, or even towns
(and long, long before there was Marjorie), people worked
at fitting shapes together to fill in a whole surface.

Here they tried it with three-sided
shapes on a block of ochre.

77,000 YEARS AGO

Here with four-sided shapes on
a piece of ostrich eggshell.

60,000 YEARS AGO

And here with six-sided
shapes on a mammoth tusk.

17,000 YEARS AGO

Soon Marjorie discovered that some shapes mean sounds. How incredible that all stories were made out of just twenty-six shapes. She pored over books until she could read every word.

So when, at only five years old, she walked to the Garden Valley School, the teacher placed her in the second grade. This made her feel quiet and like she didn't quite fit.

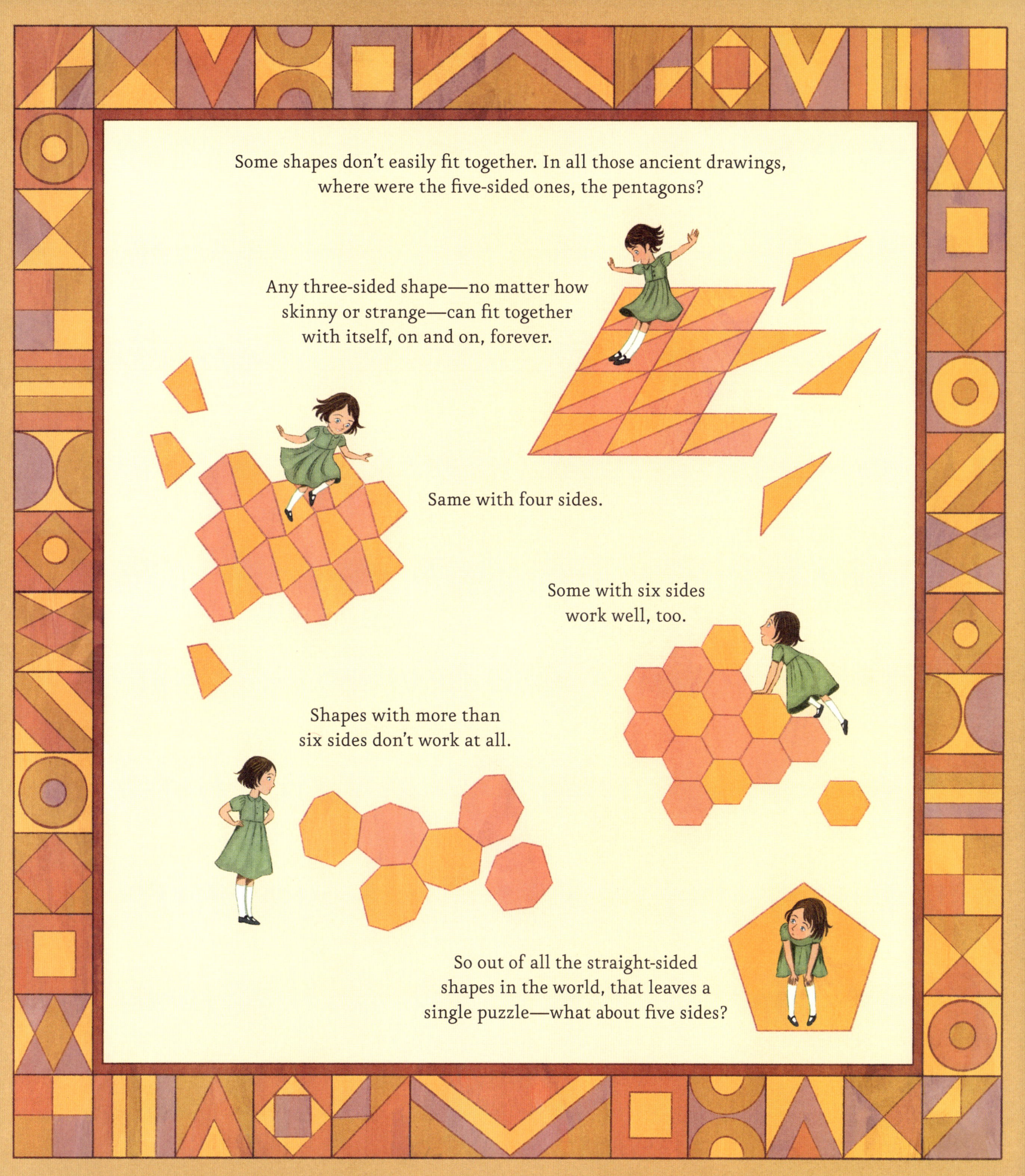

Some shapes don't easily fit together. In all those ancient drawings, where were the five-sided ones, the pentagons?

Any three-sided shape—no matter how skinny or strange—can fit together with itself, on and on, forever.

Same with four sides.

Some with six sides work well, too.

Shapes with more than six sides don't work at all.

So out of all the straight-sided shapes in the world, that leaves a single puzzle—what about five sides?

One time, when Marjorie was feeling quiet, her teacher showed her the golden rectangle. Marjorie was wonderstruck.

It lay like a hidden map—always with the same perfect proportions—underneath sunflowers and shells and webs. Some shapes were so beautiful they made her want to be an artist.

Artists are in the business of making shapes.
So the problem of five sides fascinated them.

But no matter how they placed it, a regular
pentagon made gaps or overlaps.

Four and six sides work.

And five is right between.

So there has to be a way!

They squeezed and tugged pentagons until,
finally, they found one that fit together
with copies of itself.

It fit so beautifully that they
carved it into screens and made tiled floors.

Later, Marjorie longed to study art and geometry, to be in the business of making shapes. Her parents, however, thought she should become a secretary. So in junior high, she practiced typing, which she didn't like at all.

But one teacher noticed Marjorie's longing and made her the Lunch Hour Librarian of Magazines. Now Marjorie could read to her heart's content—all about honeybees and sea creatures and roses—and dream of making beautiful things.

But beautiful tilings didn't really solve the problem of five.
How many different *kinds* of pentagons could tile a floor?
Now mathematicians were intrigued.

And in 1918, Karl Reinhardt made a list of one,
two, three, four, five different types of tiling
pentagons. He thought he had them all.

1   **2**   **3**   **4**   **5**

Each pentagon could
create a pattern. Bow ties
and nodding knights.

Honeycombs and windmills and blooms.

His list is no
doubt complete!

Much, much later, living in California, now with one, two, three, four, five children of her own, Marjorie learned something else about shapes. Even if you haven't studied art or math, even if you've never gone to college, you can make shapes yourself and change how the world looks.

Marjorie's house was up high and a canyon lay behind. She yearned to go down into it, so she stared at the canyon until she figured out how.

Every day, month after month, without asking anyone for help, she shaped the earth into a path, dug it up and moved it, until she could zigzag all the way down from the top to the bottom.

It's hard to discover a shape, to make it yourself.
As it turns out, Reinhardt may have just gotten tired.

Richard Kershner was also obsessed with the problem of five.

Kershner worked at it for thirty-five years until he finally discovered three more types.

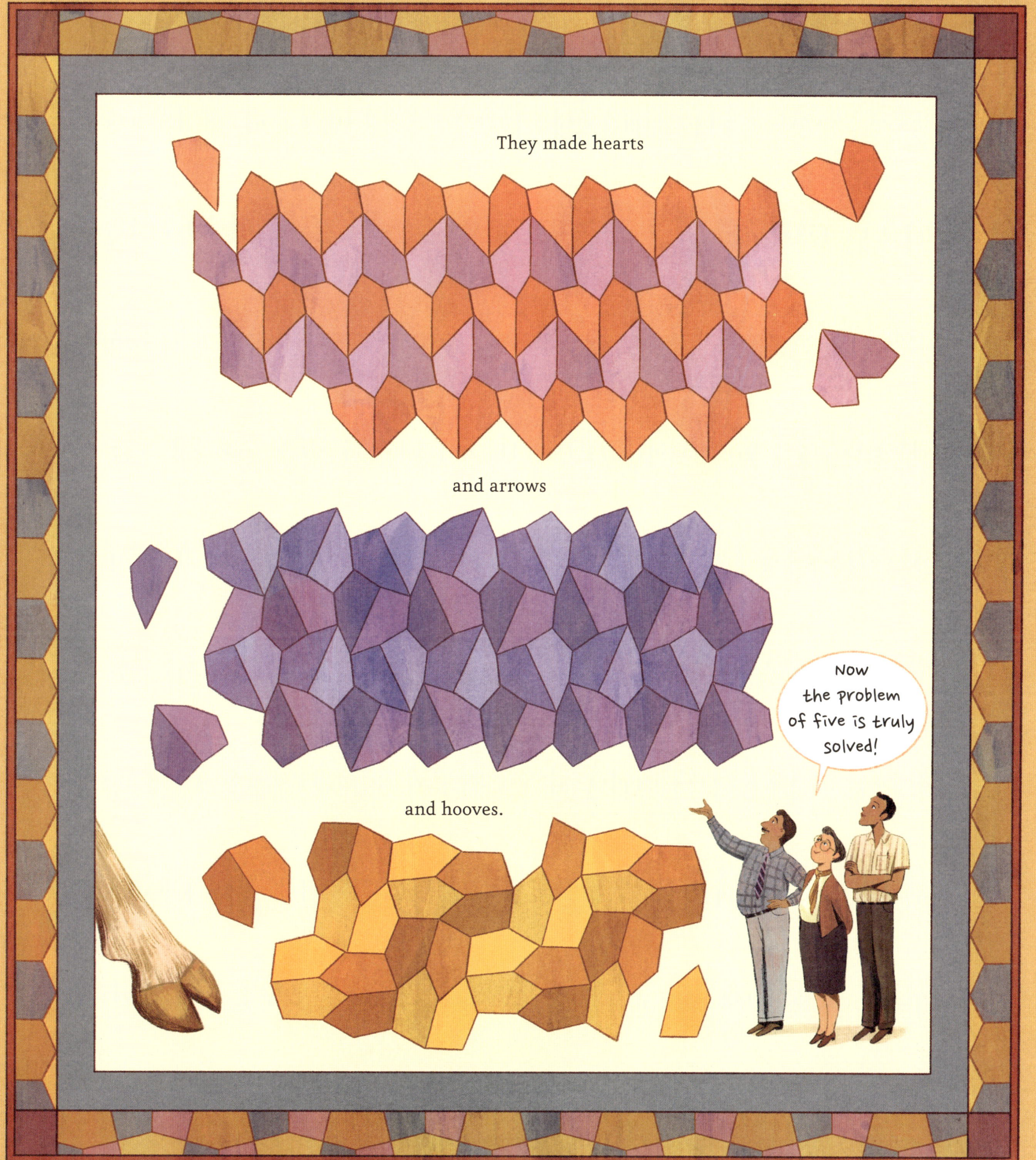

They made hearts

and arrows

and hooves.

Now the problem of five is truly solved!

With five growing children, Marjorie had a problem. There was little time to fit anything in, but she still longed to make beautiful things, to think about art and geometry. She had to find a way.

Once, she took a painting course and practiced by the sea.

Once, she followed her oldest son's math class in school, though soon she fell behind.

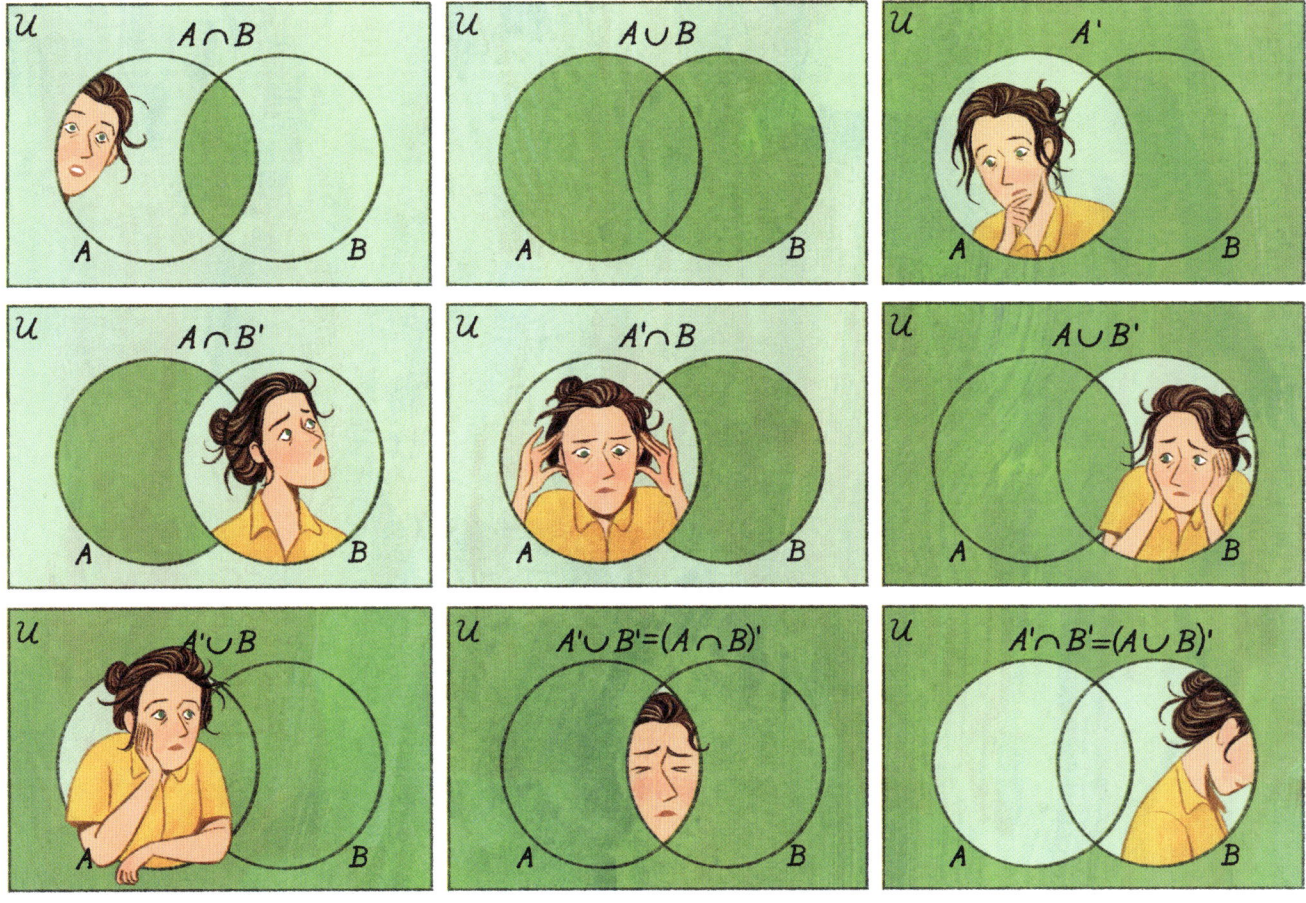

And always when her youngest son's *Scientific American*
magazine would arrive in the mail, she'd get to it first.

As if she were that lunch hour librarian again, she'd go off alone,
turn to Martin Gardner's column, Mathematical Games, and imagine.

"Imagine," Gardner started out his July 1975 column, "that you have an infinite supply of jigsaw puzzle pieces, all identical."

If you can fit them together without gaps or overlaps, you hold in your hand one of the most amazing shapes in all the world.

A shape that tiles, or tessellates, can make an endless puzzle all by itself.

Gardner went through the whole grand story of five sides.

From ancient times . . .

all the way up to Reinhardt and Kershner.

He even included a drawing by M. C. Escher of a
single tadpole that could fit into itself forever and ever.

Maybe it was math and art together, or those two marvelous ideas—
fitting and *forever*—but quiet, wonderstruck, earth-moving Marjorie was
drawn in . . . to a story that had begun eons before she was born.

How wonderful
it must have been
to discover new
types of pentagon
tiles!

Five months later, with husband and children off at work or school, Marjorie went to the mailbox. And there it was again. *Scientific American*, December 1975.

This time, right in the middle of page 117 was an announcement.

The problem of pentagons is not solved after all. A reader has found one more!

Marjorie sat and stared.

This shape could have been discovered by ancient people but has likely never been seen before by human eyes.

Marjorie had never gone to college. Her children knew more math than she did. But still, she couldn't help it. A beautiful, brave idea began to take shape in her mind.

what if I could find still another type?

She took out a blank page.
How did those mathematicians do it?

No, that was not the right question.
How would *she* do it?

Well, what *is* a pentagon? It's a shape with five sides.
Marjorie drew a little house.

Now, how to use this same little house as a blueprint for each type?
She studied the nodding knights.

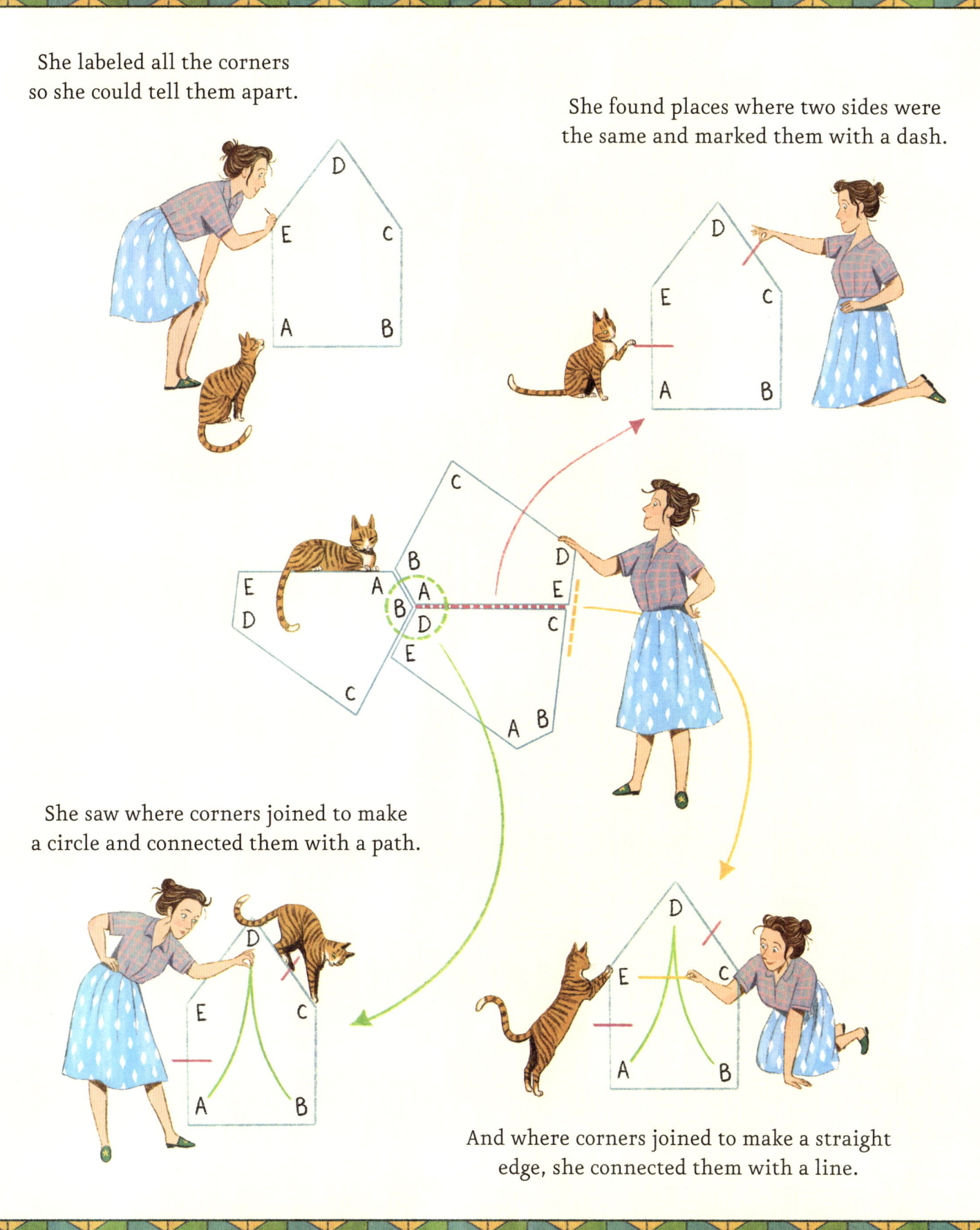

She labeled all the corners so she could tell them apart.

She found places where two sides were the same and marked them with a dash.

She saw where corners joined to make a circle and connected them with a path.

And where corners joined to make a straight edge, she connected them with a line.

Now each little house was a key to each pattern, showing exactly how the corners and sides had to fit together. She went through all the known pentagons and then began designing more.

She made a long, long list of houses and didn't get tired and didn't give up.

She scribbled them on kitchen tiles while stirring soup.

She scribbled them on scraps of paper and hid them in her Bible. She didn't say a word to anyone.

When she found a particularly
promising one, unlike all the others,

she'd measure and adjust,

turn it into a crooked
little house, until one day . . .

it worked!

There was an entire crooked little town, with no gaps
or overlaps. Everything fit, forever and ever.
Had she done it?

Professor S. and Marjorie
began writing letters back and forth.

Marjorie sent stacks of sketches.
The professor sent articles about shapes.

One article, written by Professor S. herself, gave Marjorie a brilliant idea.
Take two hexagons already stuck together and divide each one in half.

Now you have four pentagons.

Marjorie pored over these new pentagons. She made more lists and more crooked little towns. And in December 1976, just one year after reading Gardner's announcement, she sent Professor S. another set of sketches.

Indeed, she has discovered types 11 and 12!

And by December 1977, Marjorie had discovered type 13.

Sometimes Marjorie got tired. It's hard work discovering shapes.

But then a marvelous new idea would occur to her and she'd be back at it.

Pentagons are not so easy to lay aside.

And another thick envelope would arrive at the doorstep of Professor S.

The envelopes contained wonders. Once, Marjorie discovered a different kind of pentagon—with one angle that bent in instead of out—that could make suns and spirals and snakes.

It's called a *versatile*, because it can do so much.

Once, on a trip to Turkey and Greece, Marjorie figured out a tricky pentagon pattern that would eventually become her most famous.

And once, remembering the tadpoles, remembering the wild,
Marjorie sent that same pattern but filled with roses. Another pattern,
whose sides made the golden proportion, she filled with bees and clovers.

Professor S. wrote articles and gave lectures about Marjorie and her tiling pentagons.

And finally, in 1995, she invited Marjorie and her husband to attend
a Mathematical Association of America meeting.

And so, quiet, wonderstruck, earth-moving, shape-discovering Marjorie stood up.
All the mathematicians in the room immediately rose from their seats, too,
and cheered her with thunderous applause.

They cheered because Marjorie showed them what it really means to be a mathematician.
They cheered because she was an amateur, not a professional.

She hadn't done all this work to get a better job or money or fame.
For decades, Marjorie Rice had pursued the problem of *fitting* and *forever* out of love.

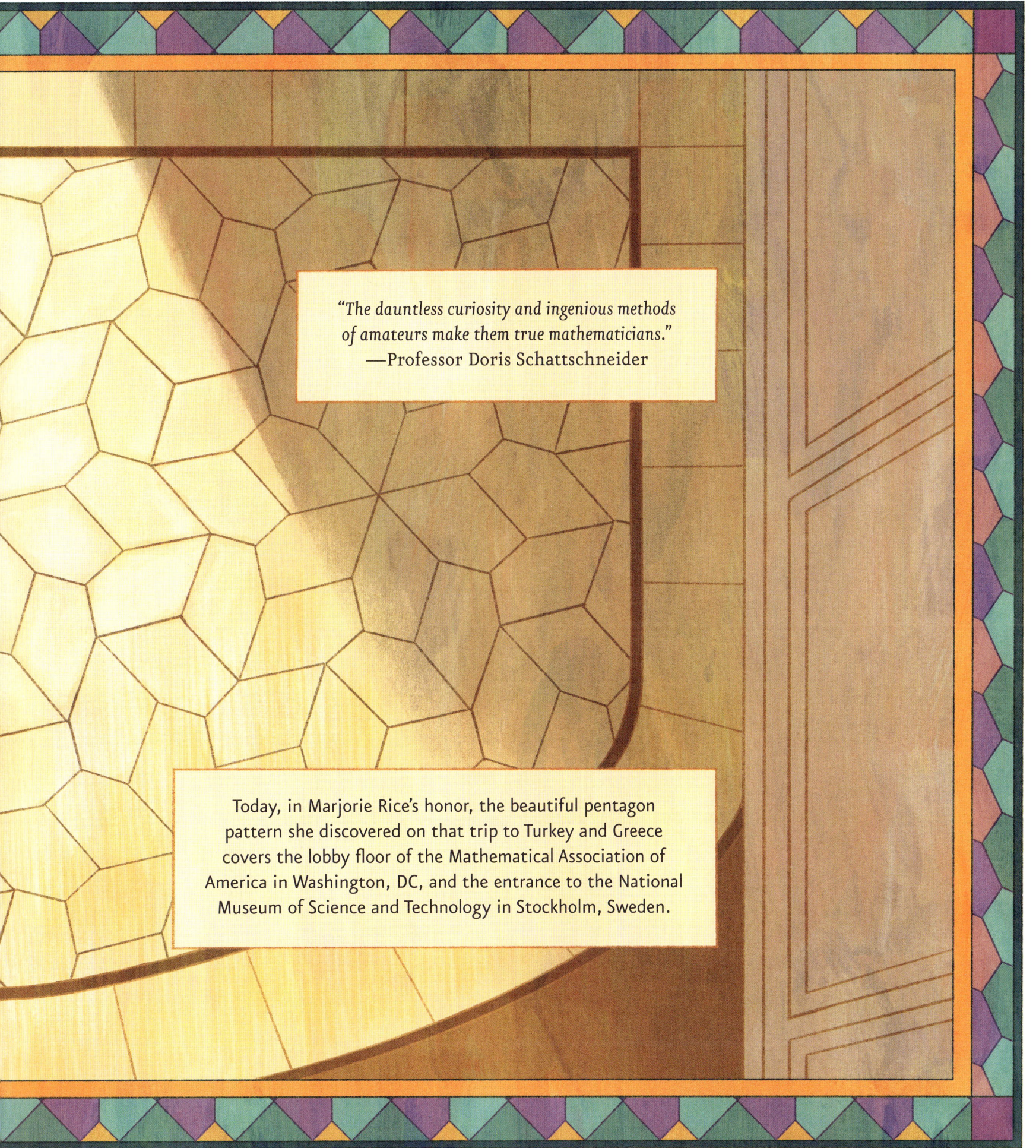

"The dauntless curiosity and ingenious methods of amateurs make them true mathematicians."
—Professor Doris Schattschneider

Today, in Marjorie Rice's honor, the beautiful pentagon pattern she discovered on that trip to Turkey and Greece covers the lobby floor of the Mathematical Association of America in Washington, DC, and the entrance to the National Museum of Science and Technology in Stockholm, Sweden.

Author's Note

Though I didn't know it then, when I was a little girl I touched a piece of Marjorie Rice's story. From 1977 to 1978, I lived in Australia with my family, going to school, eating Vegemite sandwiches, and trying to spot kangaroos and koalas and all kinds of beautiful birds. Our closest Australian friend and host, Michael Hirschhorn, was my father's mathematics graduate student. I remember him proudly showing us a beautiful, circular rug. He had hooked the rug from a single, equilateral tiling pentagon that he'd discovered himself.

Decades later, I found out that in that same year, the year Marjorie had discovered the thirteenth pentagon type, the year I'd lived in Australia, Michael Hirschhorn shared his discoveries with Marjorie Rice! He, too, had been obsessed with the problem of five. Hirschhorn is actually the one who came up with that wonderful term—*versatile*—which Marjorie Rice had used to describe some of her own discoveries.

When I was working on this book, I was fascinated to find out that my father, George Andrews, and Doris Schattschneider (Professor S.) have known each other for a long time. I eventually met Professor S., who helped me understand Marjorie's pentagons. I also met two of Marjorie's children—her oldest son, David, and youngest daughter, Kathy—both of whom spoke with great love and admiration about their brilliant and kind mother. In a recent correspondence with David, I learned a beautiful final story about Marjorie.

After Marjorie died and her children were going through her things, David found an odd little contraption made of wood and netting. He soon realized it was a gentle trap for spiders that Marjorie had fashioned so she could safely carry them outside. Marjorie loved nature in general, but I imagine she must have felt a particular kinship with those small, eight-legged creatures in her home who, like her, spent much of their time quietly spinning shapes in secret.

Is the Story of Five Over?

The historic problem Marjorie solved was specifically about *convex* pentagons, shapes that aren't dented (or concave) like these:

Except for the versatile, almost all of the pentagons in this book are convex. Marjorie Rice's discovery of four new types of convex tiling pentagons brought the total of tiling pentagon types to thirteen. (Her first find was the tenth type discovered, but it is officially known as type 9 due to its similarity to type 8.) But the question remained: Were there still more types? No one knew. Anyone who looked was like an explorer searching for an island that might not even be there.

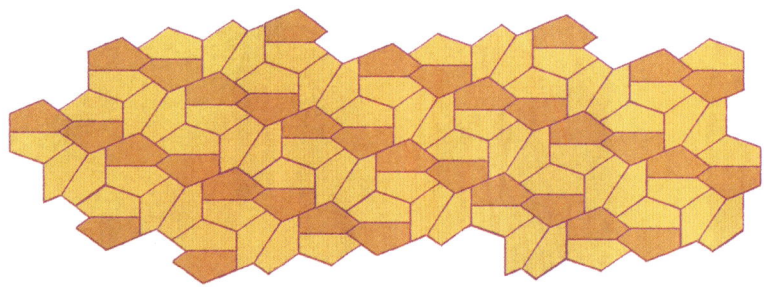

Well, in 1985, almost a decade after Marjorie's discoveries, Rolf Stein struck land and discovered type 14. Then thirty whole years went by with no further discoveries. Finally in 2015, a group of three mathematicians (Casey Mann, Jennifer McLoud-Mann, and David Von Derau), with the help of a computer, discovered the fifteenth and last tiling pentagon. But they didn't know for sure it was the last until two years later when Michaël Rao, also with the help of a computer, proved that their discovery was in fact the final one. And so, the ancient puzzle and story came to a close.

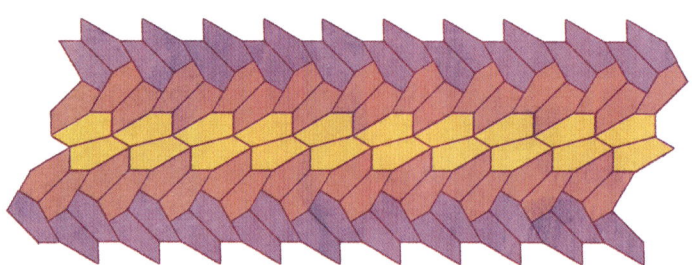

How to Discover a Shape

But the story of shapes is never really over! Here's a list of ways you can enter the story yourself:

Draw. Draw Anything. Drawing is the art of making shapes. Every time you draw, you are creating new, never-before-seen shapes. Get the book *Drawing with Children* by Mona Brookes, which teaches you how to draw by seeing and sketching shapes.

Explore Three-Sided Shapes. Every triangle—every single one—can fit together with copies of itself with no gaps or overlaps. So every triangle tiles, or tessellates. Try it. Draw a triangle, any triangle, on a piece of heavy paper. Use a ruler so the sides are perfectly straight and meet neatly at the corners. Chances are that no one has ever drawn exactly this triangle before! Now cut out your triangle and trace it over and over, fitting it together with its copies, making an endless puzzle out of just this one shape.

Explore Four-Sided Shapes. Repeat the previous exercise but with quadrilaterals (*quad* means four, *lateral* means side). Again, any quadrilateral will tessellate. Even some mathematicians don't realize that all quadrilaterals (even dented ones) can tile.

Look for Tilings in the World. Six-sided shapes are trickier because there are only three types of hexagons that tile. But tilings by hexagons are actually some of the most commonly seen in the world. Look for tessellations—of triangles, quadrilaterals, hexagons, even pentagons—on floors, pavements, mosaics, honeycombs, buildings, paths. Oh, and mammoth tusks! Take an expedition to photograph all the geometric tilings in your world.

Explore Pentagons. While I was writing this book, I spent hours playing with Christopher Danielson's Gallon of Pentagons—twelve beautiful wooden copies of each of the fifteen pentagon types—trying to figure out how each type tiles. You can print out these pentagon shapes here: bit.ly/4bJt07v

Go Beyond the Standard Shapes. There are plenty of other ways to continue your explorations!

⬡ Find books about or by M. C. Escher. Get inspiration from all of his amazing tessellations.

⬠ Find books by Martin Gardner. He wrote a lot about tessellations but also about all sorts of mathematical puzzles.

⬠ Play with the app at www.conwaysmagicalpen.com. Professor S. helped create this! This app will allow you to design all sorts of surprising tessellations.

⬠ Get the fascinating book *Tessellations: Mathematics, Art, and Recreation* by Robert Fathauer. It's full of ideas, explanations, pictures, and endless activities for families or classrooms.

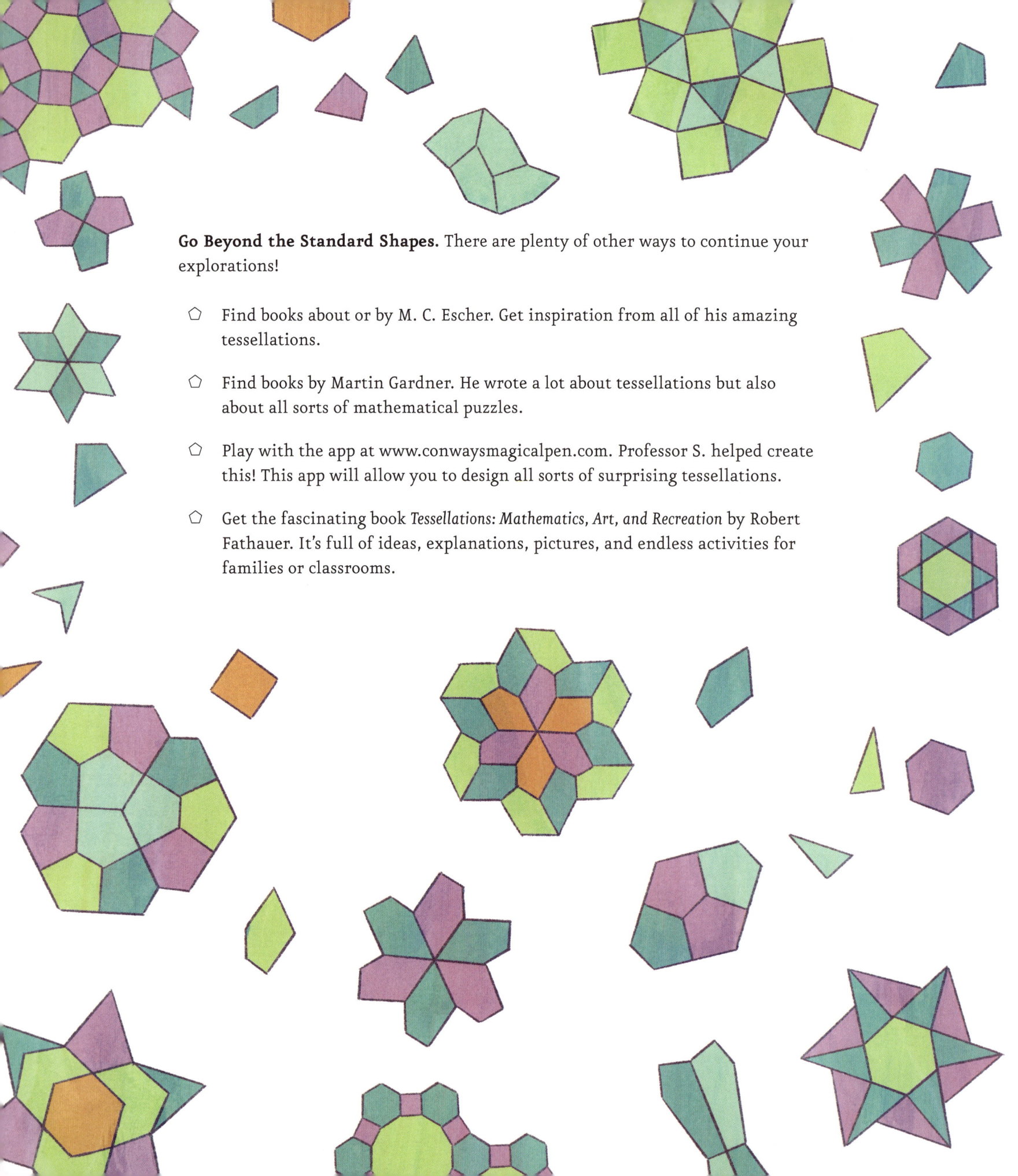

Select Bibliography

Gardner, Martin. "A Random Assortment of Puzzles, Together with Reader Responses to Earlier Problems." Mathematical Games, *Scientific American*, December 1975, 116–119.

———. "On Tessellating the Plane with Convex Polygon Tiles." Mathematical Games, *Scientific American*, July 1975, 112–119.

Rice, Marjorie. "Escher-Like Patterns from Pentagonal Tilings." In *M. C. Escher's Legacy: A Centennial Celebration*, edited by Doris Schattschneider and Michele Emmer, 244–251. Berlin: Springer-Verlag, 2003.

———. Unpublished correspondence with Doris Schattschneider, Eugene Strens Recreational Mathematics Collection, University of Calgary Library.

Schattschneider, Doris. "In memoriam: Marjorie Rice (16 February 1923–2 July 2017)." *Journal of Mathematics and the Arts* 12, nos. 2–3 (2018), 51–54. https://doi.org/10.1080/17513472.2017.1399680.

———. "In Praise of Amateurs." In *The Mathematical Gardner*, edited by David A. Klarner, 140–166. Boston: Prindle, Weber & Schmidt, 1981.

———. "Marjorie Rice and the MAA Tiling." *Journal of Mathematics and the Arts* 12, nos. 2–3 (2018), 114–127. https://doi.org/10.1080/17513472.2018.1453740.

Schattschneider, Doris, and Marjorie Rice. "The Incredible Pentagonal Versatile." *Mathematics Teaching* 93 (1980), 52–53 and cover.

Singh, Sunil, and Dr. Christopher Brownell. *Math Recess: Playful Learning in an Age of Disruption*. London: IMPress, 2019.

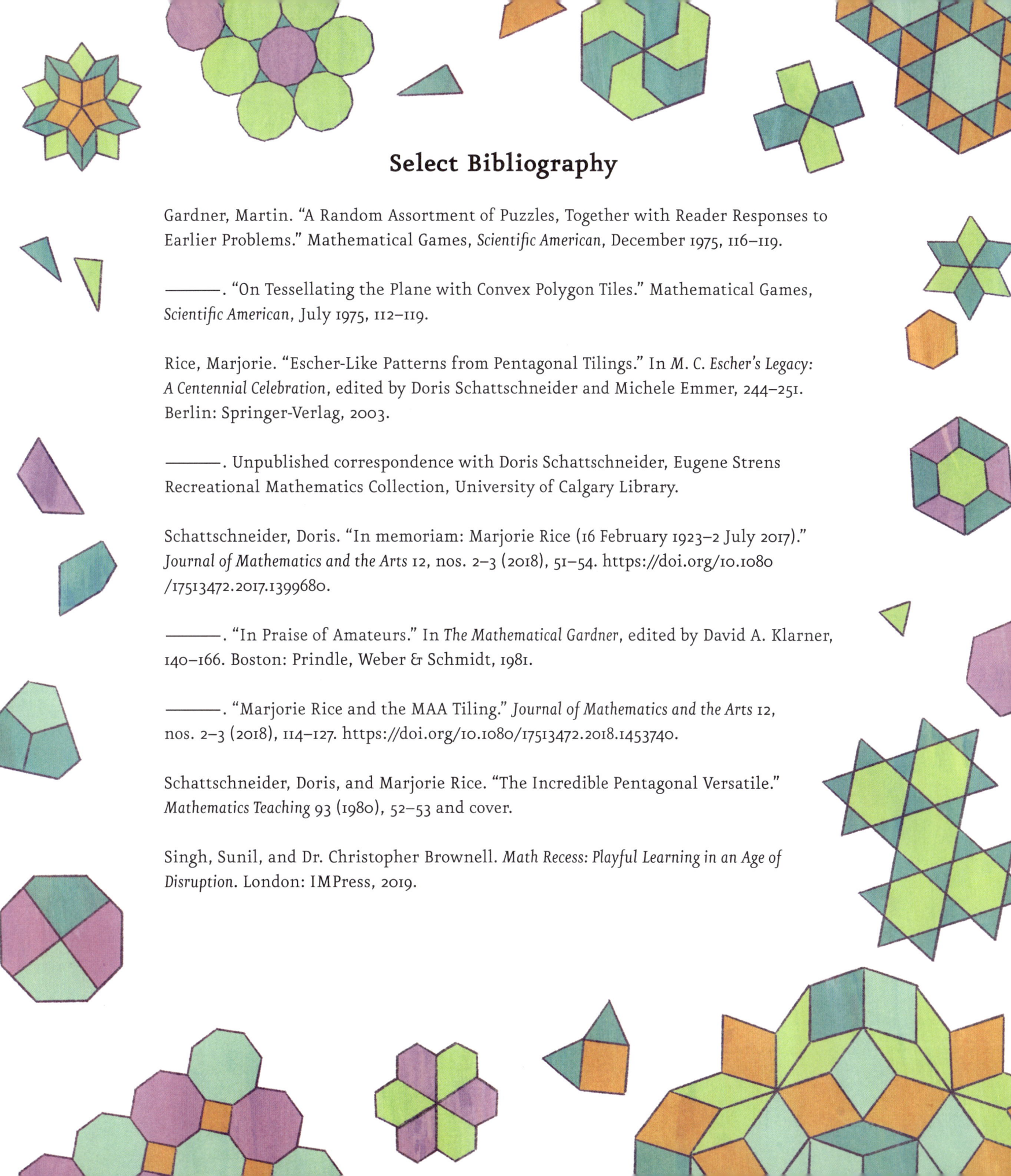

For Marjorie Rice and for all the amateur mathematicians out
there who remind us what it means to love what we do
AA

To my grandmother Lia, who valued art just as much as mathematics
AB

Marjorie as a little girl out in
nature with . . . a cat!

Doris Schattschneider (far right) with Gilbert and
Marjorie Rice at the MAA meeting in 1995.

A special thank-you to Doris Schattschneider for her gracious and invaluable
help in the research for this book and also the eventual editing process.
Professor S. is an accomplished mathematician herself, an innovative expositor
of the work of M. C. Escher, and, of course, the person who helped support
Marjorie Rice's passion for geometry and give her a voice in the world.

About the illustrations:
One of the beautiful aspects of tessellating shapes is that they can become a grid for designing repeating images.
On the page with the roses, bees, and clover, the art within the tiling was created by Marjorie Rice.
On page with the fish, raccoons, and moths, Anna Bron created her own tessellating images.

The tadpole tessellation was inspired by an M. C. Escher drawing.

Candlewick Press, 99 Dover Street, Somerville, Massachusetts 02144. www.candlewick.com.
Printed in Shenzhen, Guangdong, China. 25 26 27 28 29 30 CCP 10 9 8 7 6 5 4 3 2 1